Contents

Page

NELSON MANDELA

Oliver Tambo was Mandela's friend. They started a law business together in 1952 and fought for black rights in South Africa.

Nelson Mandela in 1937, at the age of nineteen.

Winnie Mandela became Mandela's second wife in 1958. She supported him during his long years in prison.

MR F.W. DE KLERK

F. W. de Klerk was President of South Africa from 1989 to 1994. He understood that South Africa had to change. He freed Mandela from prison.

Graça Machel became Mandela's third wife in 1998.

Mandela with his grandchildren in 2008, on his ninetieth birthday.

PLACES

Mvezo Mandela was born in this South African village in 1918.

Qunu As a boy, Mandela lived a simple, happy life in this village.

The 'Great Place' This was the home of the King of the Thembu people. Mandela lived here when he was a teenager.

Qunu

Johannesburg

Johannesburg Mandela moved to the biggest city in the country when he was a young man. He became interested in politics here.

Robben Island This small island was the most famous prison in all of South Africa. Mandela was here for twenty-five years.

NELSON MANDELA

ANC LEADER WALKS FREE AT LAST

On February the 11th, 1990 Nelson Mandela woke up at 4.30 in the morning. All his days started at the same time in his small house in Victor Verster Prison, but that Sunday was very different. His bags were ready. Today he was leaving.

In the afternoon he got into a car with his wife Winnie. The car started driving him to the outside world. But, before the last prison door, Mandela stopped the driver. After twenty-seven years in prison he wanted to *walk* the last few metres.

Mandela held his wife's hand as he walked out. Thousands of people were waiting for him there. There were people from newspapers and television stations. 'How does it feel to be free?' they asked him. Mandela could not find the words to answer that question. He went to prison at the age of forty-five and was leaving at the age of seventy-one. What could anyone say about those lost years?

But the shouts of all those people made him strong. He closed his right hand and lifted it over his head. That was the sign of his political party, the ANC. After 10,000 days in prison, Mandela was still ready to fight for a fairer South Africa.

CHAPTER 1
Two worlds

'I don't remember any time as a child when I was alone.'

Nelson Rolihlahla Mandela was born on July the 18th, 1918, in the South African village of Mvezo. The Thembu people lived in this part of the country, and Mandela's father, Chief Gadla Mandela, was an important man to the Thembu. He was the village's leader and he also helped other leaders of the Thembu.

At that time, important Thembu men usually had more than one wife. Chief Mandela had four wives. Rolihlahla was his first son with his third wife, Nosekeni Fanny. In Xhosa, the language of the Thembu people, Rolihlahla meant 'trouble-maker'. But the boy's older sisters had a different name for him: Buti.

Buti was still very young when the family's life changed completely. There was an important white government worker in the area, and he and Chief Mandela didn't always agree. When Chief Mandela didn't follow the white man's orders one day, he lost his job and all his money. Suddenly Buti was not the son of a rich and important man any more.

This was a good example of life in South Africa at the time. In many ways, life in Mvezo was the same as life for the Thembu hundreds of years before. But the government of this part of the world was white now, and the white people did not care about the lives and rights of black South Africans.

Nosekeni Fanny and her family moved to another village, Qunu. Chief Mandela did not come with them, but he visited often.

Qunu village

In the new village the family lived on a small piece of land with three small houses. The family kept food in one and cooked in another. They slept in the last house.

The family was poor now, but Buti was a happy child. He helped to care for the family's animals. He loved to play with the other children in the village. His father spent time with the families of each of his wives. Buti loved to hear his many stories of great Thembu people in the past.

By the age of seven Buti was clearly a clever boy. Not every child went to school, but his mother decided to send Buti. But first he needed clothes for school. His father gave the young boy a pair of his own trousers. Of course, they were much too big. Buti had to do a lot of work on them before they finally fitted him.

The teachers at the school gave the children European names. Now the boy was not Buti or Rolihlahla. He was Nelson. At first he did not like this new name, but he was happy at school. But then, for the second time in his young life, everything changed completely. When he was ten years old, Nelson's father died.

Nosekeni Fanny did not want her son to spend the rest of his early years with no father in his life. It was time for him to leave Qunu. He followed his mother out of the village. They walked for more than a day until they came to Mqhekezweni. The white houses in the middle of this village were bigger and more beautiful than any in Nelson's old villages. This was the 'Great Place'. It was the home of the king of the Thembu people, Chief Jongintaba. Because Nelson's father helped him years earlier, Jongintaba wanted Nelson to live with him now.

SOUTH AFRICA
IN THE PAST

THE FIRST SOUTH AFRICANS

Before white Europeans reached South Africa, it was not one country. Many different groups of black Africans lived in this part of Africa. Each of these groups spoke their own language and had their own ways of life. Two of the biggest groups were the Zulus and the Xhosa. Nelson Mandela's Thembu people were part of the Xhosa group.

THE BOERS

In 1652, some Dutch people came to South Africa and made their home there. In the next few years, more and more people arrived, mostly from the Netherlands but also from Germany and France. They took more and more land for their farms. People later called these new white people in South Africa the 'Boers' – this was the Dutch word for farmers. There were terrible fights between the Boers and the black Africans for many years.

A fight between Boers and Zulus in 1838

THE BRITISH

In the early 1800s the British became interested in South Africa. They took the area around the Cape of Good Hope and quickly won more and more power. Many Boers moved north of the Orange River to escape the British. In the late 1800s there were two areas under Boer power: the Transvaal and the Orange Free State. But the British wanted the diamonds and gold in the Boer areas. They fought a long, hard war with the Boers from 1899 to 1902, and finally the British won power over all of South Africa.

A NEW COUNTRY

In 1910 the different areas became one country, South Africa. This was part of the British Commonwealth*.

From the start, the new white, English-speaking government was not fair to black South Africans. In Cape Province and Natal, only people with houses could vote. Most black South Africans were poor and did not own houses. Politics was even more unfair in the Orange Free State and the Transvaal. No black people could vote.

White people had almost ninety percent of the land – all the best, richest parts. Most black people did not go to school and they could not do certain jobs. Black workers got very little money. They could not travel to certain areas.

This was South Africa when Nelson Mandela was a child. Most of the people in the country were black but white people had all the power.

* The British Commonwealth is a group of countries that the British once governed.

What do these words mean? You can use a dictionary.

diamonds   farm   gold   power

CHAPTER 2
From boy to man

'A new world opened before me.'

Life in his new village was very different for Nelson. He had a bed for the first time. He saw a car for the first time, too. He started to wear European clothes. He also had a new friend. His name was Justice and he was Chief Jongintaba's son. Nelson went to a new school. Here his lessons included English and Xhosa, the language of his people.

Nelson learned a lot at the Great Place. He watched Chief Jongintaba in his job as the king of the Thembu people. When somebody had a problem, he came to the king. Everybody could speak freely. Jongintaba always listened quietly. Then he tried to give an answer that was fair to everybody. Jongintaba was a good leader and Nelson learned a lot from him.

Nelson Mandela of the Thembu

Soon Nelson went to live at a different school, about a hundred kilometres from Mqhekezweni. His friend Justice was already a student there. All of the students were black, but the head of the school was a white man, Reverend Harris. The Harris family were the first white people that Nelson Mandela really knew. He was not the cleverest student in the school, but he worked hard. He enjoyed sports and became tall and strong.

At the age of twenty-one, he went to Fort Hare University. He arrived there with a new pair of shoes – a special present from Chief Jongintaba. There were about a thousand students at the university, all black South Africans.

While he was at Fort Hare, he met Oliver Tambo. Tambo was a student at the university too. The two men became good friends. Mandela's life was very different now from the lives of people in villages like Mvezo and Qunu. His hopes and dreams were different, too. He wanted to work in the government after university.

But Mandela always remembered the most important fact about life in South Africa: it was not the same for black people and white people. Sometimes he and his friends went to a restaurant on Sundays. They could not eat in the main dining room because they were black.

Mandela was learning about himself, too. Others looked to him as a leader. The food at the university was terrible and so the other students turned to Mandela for help. He tried to fight for change. The university was angry and sent Mandela away. But now Mandela understood something about himself. When he believed in something, he wanted to fight for it.

Back at the Great Place, Chief Jongintaba was an old man. Before he died, he wanted Nelson and Justice to find wives. In the past, Thembu fathers chose wives for their sons. But the two young men did not want to live in the past. They wanted to choose their own futures. 'We will marry when we are ready,' they said. 'And we will choose our own wives.'

Together, Nelson and Justice made a plan. They decided to go to the country's biggest city, Johannesburg. But how could they travel there? At the time, black people could not travel freely around the country without the right papers.

Finally, they heard about a white woman who was driving to the city. They paid her fifteen pounds – almost all of their money – to take them. Because they were black men, they had to sit in the back of the car all the way.

CHAPTER 3
The start of the fight

'There are many more hills to climb.'

Life was not easy in Johannesburg. Black people could only live in certain parts of the city called 'townships'. These were often poor places. Many people made their own houses with pieces of wood and things that they found. Not all jobs were open to black people in the city.

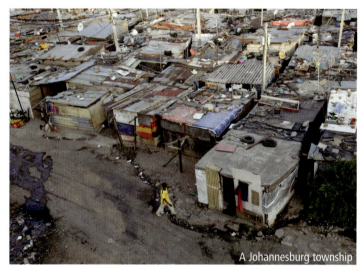

A Johannesburg township

Justice soon went back to the Great Place, but for Mandela, Johannesburg was exciting. He met a white lawyer, Lazar Sidelsky. Sidelsky was unusual because he worked for both black and white people. He liked Mandela and offered him a job in his business.

So Mandela started to work in the lawyer's office. He lived in a township that was more than ten kilometres away. Every morning, he walked all the way to his job.

Then in the evening he walked home again. All evening he studied hard because he wanted to become a lawyer himself. He didn't have a lot of money. Sometimes he didn't eat anything for days.

In 1942 he won a place at Witwatersrand University. There he could follow his dream to become a lawyer. He also met many people at the university who were interested in politics. His new friends, black and white, supported fair rights for all South Africans. Mandela agreed with them completely. Life was unfair for black South Africans – in their own country! And with no vote, how could black people ever change this unfair government?

Witwatersrand University

Mandela joined the African National Congress (the ANC). This political group fought for rights for black and other non-white Africans. But for Mandela, the group talked too much and didn't do enough. He and his friends started a smaller group, the ANC Youth League, in 1944. Mandela and his old friend Oliver Tambo worked hard for this new group.

Around this time, Mandela met a young woman. Her name was Evelyn Mase and she worked in a hospital. He and Evelyn married and they had their first son, Thembi, in 1945. Mandela was still getting a little money from his job at Sidelsky's office, but the family mostly lived on Evelyn's pay.

Mandela continued to discuss the country's political problems with his friends. How could they change things? How could they make South Africa fair for Africans?

Then, in 1948, things changed – but in the wrong way. They became much worse. The South African voters chose a new government: the National Party. This was a party of Afrikaners, and under its leader, Daniel Malan, life became even harder for non-white South Africans.

∗∗∗

Many political groups tried to fight the new government. The ANC tried to discuss black rights with them. They asked other countries for help too, but nothing worked. On May the 1st, 1950 many people in the country didn't go to work, as a protest. Mandela and his friend Walter Sisulu were walking home when they saw some of these peaceful protesters in the street. Suddenly police on horses appeared and started using guns. Nelson and Walter hid in a building. They later heard the terrible news. Eighteen of the protesters were dead.

The South African government was clearly ready to stop black rights in any way possible. Mandela worked even harder for the things that he believed in. In 1950 he became one of the leaders of the ANC.

APARTHEID

In 1948, there was a new government in South Africa – the National Party. This was a party of Afrikaners (another name for the Boers). In the eyes of the National Party, there were four races in South Africa:

- whites (These included Afrikaners and English-speakers.)
- blacks (Seventy-five percent of the people in the country were black.)
- Asians (Most of these people came from India.)
- people of mixed race

The National Party made a lot of new laws for the country's different races. All these laws together were called *apartheid*. In the Afrikaners' language, Afrikaans, this word means 'keeping away from others'.

Under apartheid:

- No black South Africans anywhere in the country could vote.

- Black and white South Africans could not marry.

- Many black South Africans had to move to 'homelands'. These were new areas for the different black South African groups, and the land in these areas was very poor. Black people needed papers to work in white towns or on white farms.

- White people and black people had completely different hospitals, schools and buses. They even had different toilets! Many places in the country – beaches, parks, libraries – had signs that said FOR WHITES ONLY.

It was a crime to break any of these new laws, and the punishments were hard. Every year the National Party added new apartheid laws. All of these laws did the same thing – they gave the best of everything to white South Africans.

What do these words mean? You can use a dictionary.
mixed   punishment   race

CHAPTER 4
Protest

'Nothing is black or white.'

In 1952, Mandela was a lawyer at last. He and his friend Oliver Tambo opened the country's first ever law business with black lawyers. At home, he and Evelyn had a second son. Then they had a daughter, but she died. They had a second daughter in 1954.

Lawyers Mandela and Oliver Tambo

Around this time, Mandela became interested in Ghandi's* fight against the British government in India. The ANC made a new plan. They wanted black South Africans to fight apartheid. Mandela travelled all around the country to ask for people's support. This was not easy.

* Mohandas Ghandi was a political leader in India. He protested peacefully against the British who governed his country.

Often he had to walk from town to town. In every place, he gave the same message: Africans had to work together for change.

✱✱✱

POLICE ARREST THOUSANDS ACROSS THE COUNTRY

The plan was simple. The ANC wanted all non-white South Africans to go into 'white only' areas. The police could not arrest *everybody*. Lots of people agreed to help with the ANC's plan. They went into 'white only' restaurants and trains and they used 'white only' toilets and waiting rooms. During six months in 1952, the police arrested 8,000 non-white South Africans in 'white only' areas. One of the 8,000 was Nelson Mandela.

The 1952 protest

He went to court, but they did not send him to prison. In the eyes of the court, Mandela's protest was peaceful. But now the government knew about him. Mandela could not travel around the country any more. He couldn't even leave the city. He couldn't work for the ANC or continue with his political activities.

But of course, Mandela did not stop. With his help, the ANC wrote to thousands of black Africans. They wanted all the different political groups against the government to join together as a new group, the Congress Alliance. The Congress Alliance wanted the same rights for all people. They wanted everybody to vote for the country's government. They wanted everybody to live and work freely and fairly.

Protests continued. But the long fight against the government was hurting Mandela's home life. By 1955 he and Evelyn were not together any more. In 1956, the police arrested Mandela and many other political leaders for 'crimes against the government'. 155 people went to court. This was much worse than Mandela's last time in court. The government could kill people for this crime. With so many people, the court took a long time to decide. Mandela had to live with this uncertain future for five years, but at the end of this time, the courts decided not to do anything.

Around the same time Mandela met another woman, Nomzamo Winifred (Winnie) Madikizela, and the two married in 1958. They had their first daughter, Zenani, the following year and their second daughter, Zindzi, the year after that.

Nelson and Winnie marry

***

69 DEAD
IN SHARPEVILLE PROTEST

All the time there were more and more protests against apartheid. But the government did not listen. In 1960 there was a protest on the streets of Sharpeville, a town near Johannesburg. The police had guns. They killed sixty-nine of the protesters and badly hurt almost two hundred more. Many died as they were running away.

The rest of the world was angry at the terrible news from Sharpeville, but the South African government did not care. When the British queen, Elizabeth II, spoke against apartheid, South Africa just left the British Commonwealth. It was now a crime to be in the ANC. The police arrested Mandela again. This time he spent five months in prison.

The Sharpeville protest

When he was free again, Mandela was a different man. Peaceful protest was not working. It was time to hit the South African government harder. He and his friend Walter Sisulu joined a new group inside the ANC, Umkhonto. This group planned to destroy things that were important to the government. They did not want to hurt people, just things. In December 1961, they put bombs in government offices for the first time.

Soon Mandela was the leader of Umkhonto. He couldn't live his usual life with Winnie and his daughters. He moved from place to place and hid from the government. Sometimes he travelled to other countries in Africa and Europe. He wanted to tell people about the terrible problems in South Africa and win their support. In Ethiopia he learned about guns and bombs.

When he returned to the country in 1962, the police arrested Mandela again. 'It was a crime when you left the country,' they told him. Mandela went to court. On November the 7th, 1962 they sent him to prison for five years.

CHAPTER 5
The dark years

'No one really knows a country until he has been inside its prisons.'

When Mandela arrived at Pretoria Prison, he had to put on prison clothes. Mandela hated these. Most of all, he hated wearing short trousers. To him, this was a clear political message. Only black prisoners had to wear 'children's clothes' like these. Life in prison was as unfair as life in the rest of South Africa. Even here, black and white South Africans did not have the same rights. So Mandela did not put on the clothes. The food was terrible too, and it was never hot. When prison guards brought him dinner, he did not eat it.

Mandela in prison

The head of the prison listened to Mandela carefully and made him an offer. He could wear long trousers and eat his own food. But there was a price to pay. Mandela could not be with any other prisoners. He had to spend all of his time alone.

Mandela agreed to this offer. For the next few weeks, he was alone in his cell for twenty-three hours a day. He did not see or hear another prisoner. He had no books, no pens or paper. There was just one small light and it was on for twenty-four hours a day. With no watch and no window, Mandela never knew the time of day. After a few weeks, he agreed to the short trousers and the bad prison food. It was more important for him to be with other people again.

Mandela only had a few months to learn about life at this prison. Then guards ordered him to collect his things. He was going to a new prison – Robben Island. This was a prison island near the city of Cape Town. It looked green and beautiful, but Mandela knew all about Robben Island. It was one of the most horrible prisons in the world.

When Mandela and the other political prisoners arrived at Robben Island, a group of white guards met them. 'You will die here!' they shouted in Afrikaans.

It was important to Mandela to start life here in the right way. When the new guards shouted at them to move faster, Mandela went slower.

Life was hard on Robben Island, but it was not all bad at first. Mandela and three other prisoners had a large cell with a shower and toilet. There were a lot of political prisoners there, and they often spoke together about the problems in South Africa.

Then, after just nine months of his five years in prison, there was terrible news. The South African police had new information which they found at the ANC's offices at Rivonia Farm. This was proof, they said, of worse crimes against the government by Mandela, Walter Sisulu, and others in the ANC. Mandela had to go to court again. He and the others could lose their lives.

In court, Mandela spoke about all the political ideas that were important to him. For four hours he talked about his dreams of a country that was free and fair for all people. He hoped to live in a country like this one day, he said. But he was also ready to die for a country like this.

Mandela's words reached people all around the world. There were a lot of protests outside the court, and he had a lot of international support too. But this could not help him now. In the eyes of the court, he was a criminal. Many people in the courtroom wanted to kill him for his crimes, but instead the court sent him and the others to prison for

Protesters outside the court

life. As the people there heard this news, Mandela looked for his wife Winnie. But the court was busy and noisy, and he was unable to see her.

✦✦✦

Mandela went back to Robben Island. Life seemed even harder there now. He later called these 'the dark years'. There was a new part of the prison, just for political prisoners. There were about twenty men in this area, and the same number of guards. The cells were very small. Mandela could lie down with his head on one wall and his feet touched the opposite wall.

On Robben Island life was the hardest for the political prisoners. The guards woke them at 5.30 every morning. Then the prisoners had to work hard, with only a short break for lunch, until 4.00 in the afternoon. They had dinner at 4.30, but it was very small. In the evening, they washed themselves with cold seawater. The day ended at 8.00 in the evening. Then at 5.30 the next morning, the same day started again.

Young people could not visit prisoners, so Mandela did not see his children for many years. When his wife Winnie could visit, there was thick glass between them. The two could never speak freely. In 1968 he heard sad news. His mother was dead. Of course, Mandela wanted to be there with his family to say goodbye. But the head of the prison said no. A year later there was more bad news. His oldest son Thembi died in a car accident. Again, Mandela could not leave the prison.

But Mandela was sure of one thing – life on Robben Island could not destroy him. He exercised every day. Many of the other prisoners thought of him as their leader. He fought hard to make prison life better for them all. Slowly, this worked. The prisoners had better food and more letters from home. Most importantly, they had books. Now they could study in their cells. They could discuss ideas together. Some people even called the prison 'Robben Island University'!

But Robben Island still had all of South Africa's political problems. 'There were no black guards and no white prisoners,' Mandela later wrote. In fact, most of the guards were Afrikaners. They ordered the prisoners to call them *baas* – 'boss'. Of course, Mandela said no. But he did not hate his guards. He even studied the Afrikaans language so he could speak to them more easily. Some of the guards liked and helped him. Mandela had his own little garden on the island. He loved growing vegetables there, and always gave them to other prisoners *and* to guards.

Mandela in his cell on Robben Island

Robben

Robben Island is about 3.3 kilometres long, and about 7 kilometres across the sea from Cape Town.

Robben Island was famous all around South Africa. When he was a boy, Mandela heard stories about it. Europeans used it as a prison from the 1600s. Over the years the island was a prison for many great black leaders who fought against the Europeans. In the 1950s, the government sent protesters there. Prisoners on the island could see Cape Town across the water. But with the strong seas in this area, nobody could swim to the city. Escape was impossible.

CAPE TOWN

QUARRIES
Mandela and the other prisoners had to break and carry rocks here. It was very hard work.

OLD PRISON BUILDINGS
Mandela lived here when he first came to Robben Island.

Island

Today Robben Island is not a prison. It has become a museum. Thousands of people visit it. They want to see the place where Nelson Mandela was in prison for so long.

NEW PRISON BUILDINGS
Mandela lived in the small cell above for most of his time on Robben Island. In the photo below, prisoners are breaking rocks from the quarries.

What do these words mean? You can use a dictionary.
quarry   rock

CHAPTER 6
'Free Nelson Mandela!'

'I dream of an Africa which is at peace with itself.'

In some ways, each day in prison seemed to last a long, long time. But in other ways, days, weeks and months went quickly for Mandela. It wasn't hard to feel very far away from the rest of the country. He wrote to people outside the prison, but this was not easy. At first, prisoners like Mandela could only write and get one letter, no more than five hundred words, every six months. Mandela found ways to send other messages out of the prison. Sometimes he wrote little messages and hid them in special places. Prisoners from other parts of the island found them and sent them for Mandela.

Of course, it was hard to get news from the outside world. Mandela liked to talk to the new young prisoners who arrived on the island. He learned more about the fight in his country. There were new political groups that were becoming angrier and angrier about apartheid. There were more and more protests.

***

PROTESTS IN SOWETO, CHILDREN DIE

In 1976, black schoolchildren were angry because they now had to have a lot of their school lessons in Afrikaans. About 20,000 students protested against this in Soweto, a big township in Johannesburg. The police arrived. When a few protesters threw things at them, they used their guns.

Soon there was blood everywhere. Thirteen-year-old Hector Pieterson was one of about 170 people that died in the protests. His photo appeared in newspapers all over the world.

Hector Pieterson in his brother's arms

For many months after that, the protests and fighting didn't stop. By the end of the year, more than six hundred people were dead.

The next year, the police arrested one of the new leaders of the protesters, Steven Biko. Biko died while he was in a police cell.

The protesters decided to fight even harder. Mandela's old group inside the ANC, Umkhonto, still did not believe in peaceful protest. In 1980 they started to use bombs again. Now even white South Africans were speaking against their government. Many countries around the world stopped doing business with South Africa.

Mandela's old friend Oliver Tambo was now the most important leader of the ANC, but he was living in England. He wanted Nelson Mandela to be free and so he spoke to as many groups as possible. He asked people and governments of all countries to protest about Mandela. In 1980 the United Nations* said the same thing: Nelson Mandela must leave prison. During the 1980s, calls to free Mandela became louder and louder around the world. Music stars even made songs against apartheid. The song 'Free Nelson Mandela' by the band The Specials was very popular in Britain. As protests grew, Nelson

London, 1986

* The countries of the world come together as the United Nations to work for world peace.

Mandela became the 'face' of the fight against apartheid to people all around the world.

At last the South African government understood that they could not stop the protests at home. Internationally, their country was more and more alone. Something had to change.

On Robben Island, Mandela was following the news from outside as much as possible. One day in March 1982, a guard told him to put all of his things into two boxes. After eighteen years, he was leaving Robben Island for another prison. There was no time even to say goodbye to his friends. Again, the government did not care about his rights.

His new home was Pollsmoor Prison in Cape Town. He missed friends from Robben Island, but life here was easier. Now he had a bed, shower and toilet. This prison even had a radio and a library. When Winnie visited him, there was no glass between them. For the first time in twenty-one years, he could hold his wife's hand. His daughter Zeni visited him too with her own daughter. Mandela saw his grandchild for the first time.

It still wasn't easy for Mandela to follow all the news from outside. What was happening with the fight to end apartheid? At the start of 1985 he had a sign. The President* of South Africa, P. W. Botha, offered to free Mandela. But Botha wanted him to put an end to all the fighting. Mandela said no. He did not want to go free in an *unfree* country. But he continued to talk to other politicians from the government. They wanted to hear his ideas now. This was a big change for the South African government and Mandela knew that.

* The president is the political leader of a country.

In 1987 Mandela became ill and spent two months in hospital. At the end of this stay, he did not go back to Pollsmoor. His new home was Victor Verster Prison. This was a very different kind of place. Now he lived in a comfortable house with three bedrooms. But, of course, the house was still inside prison walls. He was still not a free man. During his time here, he continued to have talks with the government.

Mandela with a visitor at his house in Victor Verster Prison

On Mandela's seventy-first birthday he had a wonderful surprise. All his family – his children and grandchildren – came to spend the day with him. There was a surprise in South African politics too. P. W. Botha left the government. The new leader of the country was President F. W. de Klerk. In his early political life, de Klerk supported apartheid. But South Africa could not continue with apartheid and he understood that. Things *had* to change. He freed the political prisoners of Robben Island and let the ANC have a voice again. He started to meet Nelson Mandela in prison. In February 1990, he told the country the good news: 'Nelson Mandela will soon be free!'

This was different from Botha's offer. De Klerk was talking about a new South Africa with votes for all people. Mandela could help to build this new country.

Mandela finally left prison on February the 11th, 1990. A car took him to the centre of Cape Town. On the way, he looked out of the window. People were standing by the side of the road to see him. A lot of them lifted their right hands in the sign of the ANC. But something seemed strange to Mandela. Some of those people were *white* South Africans. It gave him hope. Maybe the new South Africa really was different from the old country.

In the centre of Cape Town 100,000 more people were waiting for him. He spoke to them as a free man for the first time in twenty-seven years. He thanked everyone

for their support during those years, both in South Africa and around the world. He spoke from the heart about his hopes for South Africa. 'Don't stop the fight!' he said. 'We will walk the last mile together.'

It was a new start in his life, and it was a new start for his country too.

CHAPTER 7
Father of a new country

*'In my country we go to prison first
and then become President.'*

Mandela was free but the fight for South Africa was not at an end yet. He became one of the ANC's leaders again. 'The government has to end apartheid,' he said. De Klerk's government changed the law so all South Africans could use the same buildings. But Mandela could not be happy until everybody in his country had a vote.

In the summer of 1990, Mandela travelled to fourteen different countries. He wanted to thank people for their support. In England, he saw his old friend Oliver Tambo. In New York, he spoke to the United Nations.

Mandela in the US in 1990

Back in South Africa, the move to a new style of government was not easy. Mandela and de Klerk both worked hard to bring the country together. A lot of white South Africans did not want to lose their hold on the country. De Klerk tried to explain the need for change to them. In 1992 there was a vote just for whites. Did they still support de Klerk and his change? Sixty-nine percent said yes.

Mandela's job was even harder. The ANC wanted all the people of the country to think of themselves as South Africans first. But black South Africans were not one group. There were many different groups with different languages and ways of life. Many of these groups had different ideas about the country's future. Some wanted to make a government just for their own part of the country. Another group, the IFP – the Inkatha Freedom Party – was the political party for the Zulus. There was a lot of trouble between the IFP and the ANC, and many people died. Mandela was unsure about de Klerk's part in this fight. Did the white leader *want* all the black groups to fight? The troubles continued the next year too. In June 1992, a group of IFP men with guns killed forty-six people from the ANC. In September, the police killed twenty-nine more ANC people during a protest.

Mandela's own wife, Winnie, was part of the troubles during this time. In 1991 she had to go to court. A black teenager was dead. Did Winnie Mandela order somebody to kill him? The court sent her to prison, but she didn't stay there for long. Even before this, Nelson decided to leave his second wife. During his long time in prison, they lived different lives. After he left prison, they did not want to live together again.

✳✳✳

Mandela and de Klerk win Nobel Peace Prize

In the middle of all these troubles, Mandela and de Klerk travelled to Sweden. There they got the Nobel Peace Prize*. The two men did not agree about many things, but they still worked together for a better country. Both men believed that South Africa had to give one vote to each man and woman in the country.

It was a dangerous time for South Africa. When a white man killed ANC leader Chris Hani outside his Johannesburg home in April 1993, many people worried. South Africa seemed to be on the edge of destruction.

* A group in Sweden gives the Nobel Peace Prize to people who have done important work for world peace.

But Mandela spoke to the country on television. A white man killed Hani, he said, but a white Afrikaner woman telephoned the police about it. The police caught the killer. 'All South Africans must stand together at this time,' he told the country. They had to stand against people who wanted to destroy the hope of a free country for all.

At last the government gave a date to vote for the next government: April the 27th, 1994. Two months before that, Mandela started to travel to towns and villages all around

the country. He spoke to *all* people, not only black South Africans. He asked white South Africans not to leave the country. The people of South Africa stood together. Even after twenty-seven long years in prison, he showed no hate to the Afrikaners.

When the important day arrived, millions of people went to vote. Many of them waited for hours, but they did not care. For most black South Africans, this was the first time in their lives that they could vote for their government.

Soon everyone knew the results. The ANC took 62.7 percent of the votes. De Klerk's National Party – the old government – took 20.4 percent. It was a clear win. At the age of seventy-five, Nelson Mandela was his country's first black leader.

On May the 10th, 1994 more than 100,000 South Africans and 140 leaders from countries around the world watched as Nelson Mandela became the President of South Africa. He spoke about his dream for 'this beautiful land'. It was time to build a new South Africa.

Mandela chose two deputy presidents*. One was Thabo Mbeki, an important ANC politician. The other was the man who freed Mandela from prison – F. W. de Klerk.

Of course, the country still had a lot of problems. There was too much crime, and not enough money for most of the people. Millions of black South Africans needed better houses, better jobs. Rich white businesses had to stay in the country and make jobs and money for everyone. Mandela worked hard. Things became better, but change in the country was slow.

* A deputy president helps the President with his or her political work.

Rugby World Cup

Rugby was a popular sport in South Africa, but people saw it as a 'white' sport. Most of the players in the South African team – the Springboks – were Afrikaners.

In the years of apartheid, many countries' sports teams did not play against South Africa. But when apartheid ended, the country could play international sports again. In 1995 they even held the Rugby World Cup. Mandela saw an important way to bring the country together – through sport. He showed his support for the country's rugby team, and South Africans of every colour followed him. With this support from all of South Africa, the Springboks reached the final. They were playing New Zealand. It was a hard match, but the Springboks won 15–12!

After the match, Mandela gave the trophy to the captain of the Springboks. The President was wearing a Springboks rugby shirt and hat. It was an important moment for many South Africans. The black President was showing his support for South Africa's mostly white rugby team. It was a sign to the world that South Africans could live together happily.

Hollywood later made a film, *Invictus*, about this match, with actor Morgan Freeman as Nelson Mandela and Matt Damon as the rugby team captain.

What do these words mean? You can use a dictionary.

captain   final   rugby   trophy

CHAPTER 8
Goodbye to politics

'My long walk has not yet ended.'

In 1999, South Africa voted again for an ANC government. But Mandela, at the age of eighty-one, decided to leave politics. It was time for a younger man to be the country's leader. His deputy president Thabo Mbeki became president.

Mandela had a third wife now. Her name was Graça Machel. The two moved back to Mandela's old village, Qunu. He was able to spend time with his family. But Mandela did not stop work completely. To the rest of the world, he was still the face of the new South Africa. He travelled all around the world in support of his country. At home, he was still making South Africa a better place for everybody. One of the country's biggest problems now was AIDS* – Mandela's own son Makgatho died from

Mandela meeting a child with AIDS

* People with AIDS become very ill. Many people die from AIDS.

AIDS in 2005. Mandela wanted people to understand this problem better and fight it.

By 2004, Mandela decided to live an even quieter life. 'Don't call me – I will call you!' he told people. But he still appeared at special times for his country.

In 2010, South Africa was the home of the football World Cup. The eyes of the world were on South Africa for a month as thirty-two countries played sixty-four football matches. A lot of people visited South Africa for the first time, and everybody agreed: it was a wonderful place to play and watch football. In the end, Spain won the Cup. After the last match, Nelson Mandela and his wife Graça waved to the 85,000 people there – and to the rest of the world through television cameras. He was almost ninety-two now, and he was wearing a big coat and hat on this cold night.

Nelson and Graça at the football World Cup

His big smile sent a message around the world. Twenty years earlier, black people and white people could not sit together at a football match in South Africa. They could not play together on the same team. But look at the country now! So much was different. To many people, one man made this happen more than anybody: Nelson Mandela, the father of the new South Africa.

Nelson Mandela:

'Don't call me. I'll call you!' With these words in 2004, Nelson Mandela told the world about the end of his working life. He wanted to spend more time with his wife and his family. 'It is time for new hands,' he told the people of his country. 'It is in your hands now.'

MANDELA DAY

The United Nations has named July 18th Mandela Day. On this day, everyone in the world has to do something good for the world for sixty-seven minutes – one minute for each year of Mandela's long fight for his country.

Mandela with Bill Clinton

American President Bill Clinton strongly supported the idea of Mandela Day. More than anybody, Mandela inspired him in his life and work.

People do different things on Mandela Day. In New York one group decided to clean the city's parks. In Johannesburg a restaurant gave a party for ill children in a hospital.

46664

46664 was Nelson Mandela's prisoner number at Robben Island. Now 46664 is the name of a charity that fights AIDS. Nelson Mandela's own son died from AIDS, and Mandela has also seen the terrible results of AIDS in the rest of his country. To get money, 46664 makes and sells clothes. It also has concerts all around the world. Singers at these concerts have included Beyoncé, Will Smith and U2. Will Smith almost decided to stop working in films after he met Mandela. Mandela inspired him to fight for a better world.

Will Smith at a 46664 concert

a man for all time

Barack Obama

WORLD LEADERS

Mandela has inspired many world leaders, too. American President Barack Obama and Mandela sometimes speak on the phone. Obama has asked people to follow Mandela's example and 'give back' to their countries and to the world.

WHAT'S IN A NAME?

People and governments around the world have named things after Nelson Mandela, to remember his important work. There is a Nelson Mandela school in Berlin, Germany, a Nelson Mandela train station in Tunisia, and a Nelson Mandela Close in London. Around the world, there are more than 150 streets, buildings, schools, bridges and parks with Nelson Mandela's name.

NELSON MANDELA CLOSE N.10

Do you think Mandela Day is a good idea? What can *you* do on Mandela Day?

What do these words mean? You can use a dictionary.

charity   close   concert   inspire

49

PEACEFUL
PROTESTS

Nelson Mandela became a strong supporter of peaceful protest. These famous leaders also used peaceful protest to fight for their people's rights.

MOHANDAS GANDHI (1869–1948)

Gandhi was born in India at a time when it was under British rule. Like black South Africans, Indians did not have the same rights as their country's white rulers.

Gandhi became a lawyer and got a job in the city of Durban, South Africa. He soon learned that life was unfair for non-whites there. He organised peaceful Indian protests against South Africa's unfair laws. The police arrested him many times, but a lot of white South Africans supported his protests.

After twenty years in South Africa, Gandhi returned to India. Millions of people joined his fight for the right of Indians to rule their own country. The British government put him in prison many times, but in the end the Indians' peaceful protests were successful. In 1947, India became its own country, free from British rule. It was a difficult time, with trouble between India's Hindu and Muslim people. When Gandhi tried to make peace between the two groups, some people were angry. In January 1948, a Hindu man killed Gandhi.

Ghandi

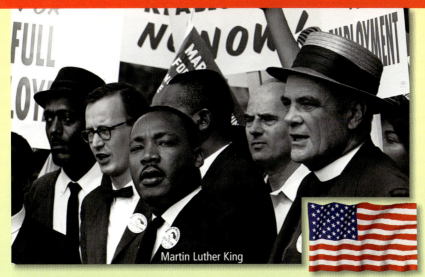
Martin Luther King

MARTIN LUTHER KING (1929–1968)

Martin Luther King fought for the rights of African Americans in the United States in the 1950s and 1960s. At this time, most African Americans in the south of the US could not vote. They could not eat in restaurants with white people. They had to stand on the bus if a white person wanted to sit in their place.

In 1955, King organised a peaceful protest against the unfair buses in Montgomery, Alabama. For 382 days, African Americans and their supporters did not use the buses, and finally there was a change in the law.

In August 1963 King was one of the leaders of a big protest in Washington DC. People all around the world heard his famous words that day – 'I have a dream.' King dreamed of an America where people of every colour had the same rights.

In 1964 he won the Nobel Peace Prize, but not everybody agreed with his message. In 1968 a white man killed him in Memphis, Tennessee.

Today Americans remember this great man on Martin Luther King Day, a day of holiday every January.

Both Gandhi and King gave their lives, but in the end their long fights for their people were successful. In other parts of the world, people are still fighting for their rights and following Gandhi and King's examples of peaceful protest.

Do you know of any other peaceful protesters? What do they protest about?

What do these words mean? You can use a dictionary.
organise   rule/ruler   successful

SOUTH AFRICA

The terrible years of apartheid have ended, and South Africa is now a popular place for holidays. It has interesting animals, high mountains and over 2,700 kilometres of coast. What can you see and do in this beautiful country?

CAPE TOWN

This is South Africa's second biggest city, and the most popular place in all of Africa for holiday-makers. Near Cape Town there are some beautiful beaches. Some are on the Indian Ocean and have warm seas. Others are on the Atlantic Ocean and have colder seas. Table Mountain, just outside the city, is 1084 metres high. Its name comes from its unusual flat top. You can walk to the top of this famous mountain. You can also take a boat to visit South Africa's most famous prison, Robben Island. It is now a museum.

ANIMALS

South Africa is home to a lot of different kinds of animal. You can see many of them at the Kruger National Park. This park has helped to save the white rhino from extinction. More white rhinos live here than in any other place in the world.

WHALE WATCHING

Hermanus is a small town on the coast of South Africa. People voted it the best place in the world to watch whales from the land. On a good day people can see seventy whales from Hermanus. There is even a 'whale crier' in the town. This person listens to the whale song and explains it to visitors!

FOOD

Because of all the different groups of people in South Africa, there are many different favourite foods. One of them is *biltong*, a kind of dry meat. It is good to eat as a snack. People also eat a lot of *braai*. This is the Afrikaans word for food that you cook outside over a fire. The country usually has good weather, so cooking and eating outside is easy!

Would you like to visit South Africa? What would you like to do there?

What do these words mean? You can use a dictionary.

coast   extinction   rhino   snack

CHAPTERS 1–2

Before you read

You can use your dictionary for these questions.

1 Use these words to complete the sentences.

crime   law   marry   politics   prison   support   village

a) He killed a man and went to _____ for twenty years.

b) They lived in a small _____ of about a hundred houses.

c) She works in _____ because she wants to help her country.

d) They were in love and decided to _____.

e) It is a terrible _____ to kill somebody.

f) If you break the _____, you'll be in trouble with the police.

g) Lots of people _____ his ideas for change in the country.

2 Answer the questions.

a) What are the main **political parties** in your country?

b) Who are the **leaders** of these parties?

c) Who **governs** your country at the moment?

d) Who can **vote** for the government?

e) What **rights** does everyone in your country have?

After you read

3 Match the place names with the sentences.

Mvezo   Qunu   The Great Place   Fort Hare University

a) Mandela met Oliver Tambo here.

b) Mandela's father was the leader of this place.

c) Mandela cared for his family's animals here.

d) Nelson lived here with Chief Jongintaba.

4 Are these sentences true or false? Correct the false sentences.

a) 'Buti' was the name of Nelson Mandela's sister.

b) Mandela's family became poor because his father died.

c) The Europeans lived in South Africa before the Zulus and the Xhosa.

d) Only a few black people could vote in South Africa.

e) Most black children went to school.

f) Justice was Chief Jongintaba's son and Nelson's friend.

g) It was easy for black people to travel around South Africa.

CHAPTERS 3–5

Before you read

5 Use the words to answer the questions.

arrest bomb cell court destroy guard peaceful protest

a) Who works in a prison?

b) Where does a lawyer work?

c) What do the police do when somebody breaks the law?

d) What can kill a lot of people?

e) What is a small room in a prison?

f) What can a fire do to a building?

g) What is a person who never wants to hurt anybody?

h) How can people tell their government that they are unhappy about something?

After you read

6 Match the two halves of the sentences.

a) Evelyn Mase

b) Umkhonto

c) The ANC

d) Daniel Malan

e) Lazar Sidelsky

f) The National Party

i) was the first political group that Mandela joined.

ii) gave Mandela a job at his law business.

iii) put bombs in government offices.

iv) was the leader of the National Party.

v) was Nelson's first wife.

vi) was a political group that made life much harder for black people.

7 Put these events in the correct order.

a) The court sent Mandela to prison for five years.

b) Nelson married Winnie.

c) The police killed sixty-nine people at Sharpeville.

d) Mandela went to Witwatersrand University.

e) Mandela became a lawyer.

f) Black people went into 'white only' areas in protest against apartheid.

8 What was hard about life as a political prisoner on Robben Island?

CHAPTERS 6–8

Before you read

9 Guess the answers to these questions, then read and check.

    a) How did Mandela leave prison? Did he escape, or did the government free him?

    b) How did these people help Mandela?

      F. W. de Klerk   Oliver Tambo

    c) Did Mandela want white people to leave South Africa?

After you read

10 Answer these questions.

    a) Why did schoolchildren protest in Soweto in 1976?

    b) Where did Oliver Tambo live in the 1980s?

    c) P. W. Botha offered to free Mandela from prison. Why did Mandela not agree?

    d) How did Nelson's life change at Victor Verster Prison?

    e) What was Nelson's surprise for his seventy-first birthday?

11 Choose the correct word.

    a) The political party of the Zulus, the IFP, **supported** / **didn't support** Mandela.

    b) **Nelson** / **Winnie** had to go to prison for a short time because of a dead black teenager.

    c) The Springboks rugby team was mostly **black** / **white**.

    d) The Springboks **won** / **didn't win** the rugby World Cup.

    e) In 2010 the **rugby** / **football** World Cup was in South Africa.

12 Are these sentences true or false? Correct the false sentences.

    a) Mandela and de Klerk won the Nobel Peace Prize together.

    b) Mandela was South Africa's first president.

    c) Mandela has had two different wives.

    d) Mandela's daughter died from AIDS.

    e) Mandela spends a lot of time in his old village, Qunu.

13 What do you think? Why do South Africans call Nelson Mandela 'the father of the new South Africa'?